HAPPY CHINESE NEW YEAR
新年快乐

A LITTLE GIRL NAMED MEI

WHO LIVED IN A SMALL VILLAGE IN CHINA

SHE WAS VERY EXCITED BECAUSE IT
WAS ALMOST TIME FOR CHINESE
NEW YEAR, THE MOST
SPECIAL HOLIDAY OF THE YEAR.

CHINESE NEW YEAR IS A TIME WHEN
FAMILIES COME TOGETHER TO CELEBRATE
THE START OF THE NEW YEAR.

IT IS A TIME FOR GIFT GIVING

EATING SPECIAL FOODS
LIKE DUMPLINGS, SPRING ROLLS,
NOODLES, STEAMED FISH,
RICE CAKE, FRUIT

AND PERFORMING TRADITIONAL
RITUALS TO BRING GOOD LUCK
IN THE COMING YEAR.

MEI HELPED HER FAMILY PREPARE FOR
CHINESE NEW YEAR BY CLEANING
THE HOUSE FROM TOP TO BOTTOM.

SHE WANTED TO MAKE SURE
THAT EVERYTHING WAS SPARKLING
CLEAN TO WELCOME THE NEW YEAR.

SHE ALSO HELPED HER FAMILY DECORATE THE HOUSE WITH RED LANTERNS AND PAPER CUTTINGS, WHICH ARE BELIEVED TO BRING GOOD LUCK.

ON THE DAY OF CHINESE NEW YEAR,
MEI GOT DRESSED IN HER FINEST CLOTHES
AND GATHERED AROUND THE TABLE WITH
HER FAMILY TO ENJOY A SPECIAL FEAST.

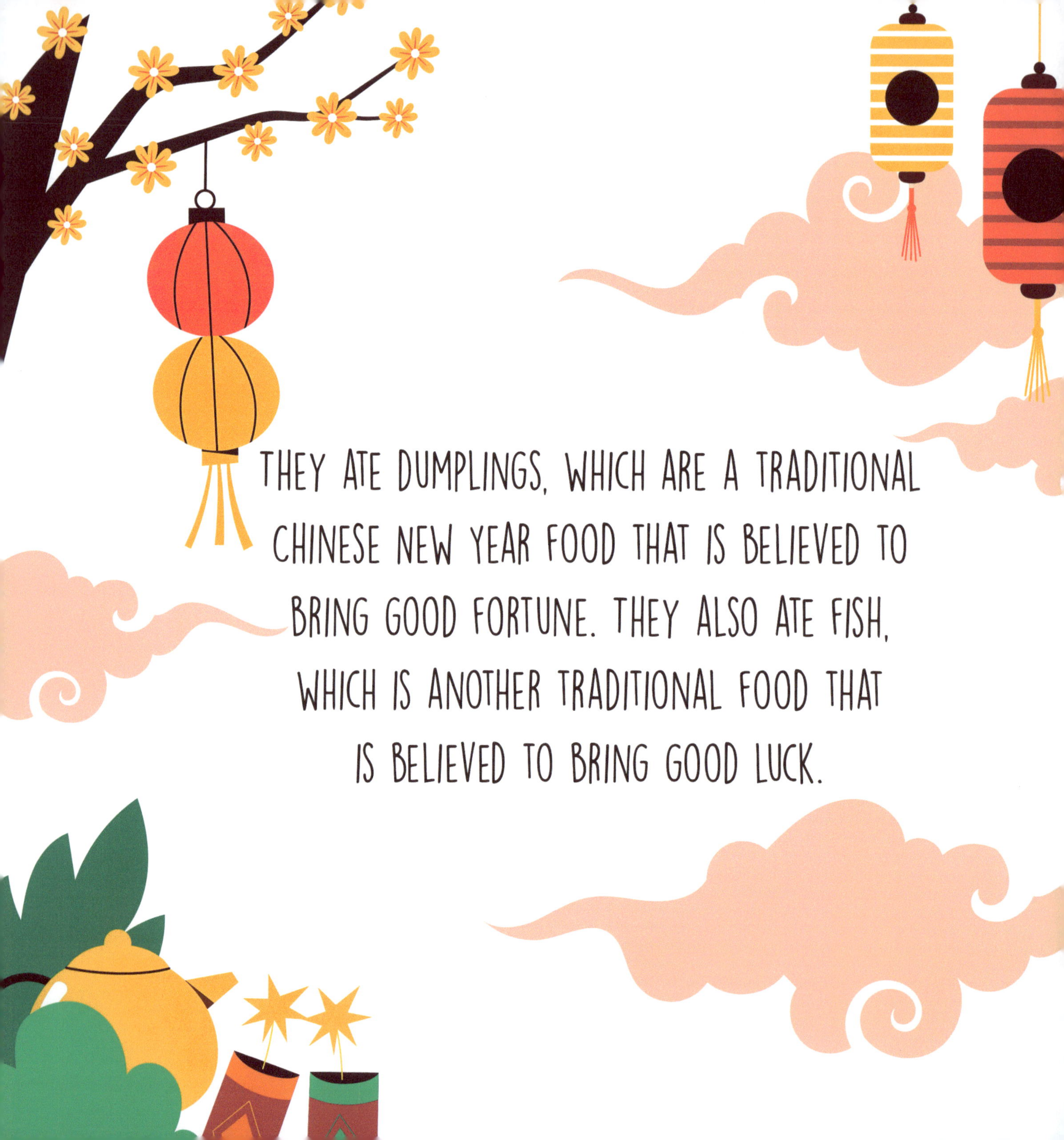

They ate dumplings, which are a traditional Chinese New Year food that is believed to bring good fortune. They also ate fish, which is another traditional food that is believed to bring good luck.

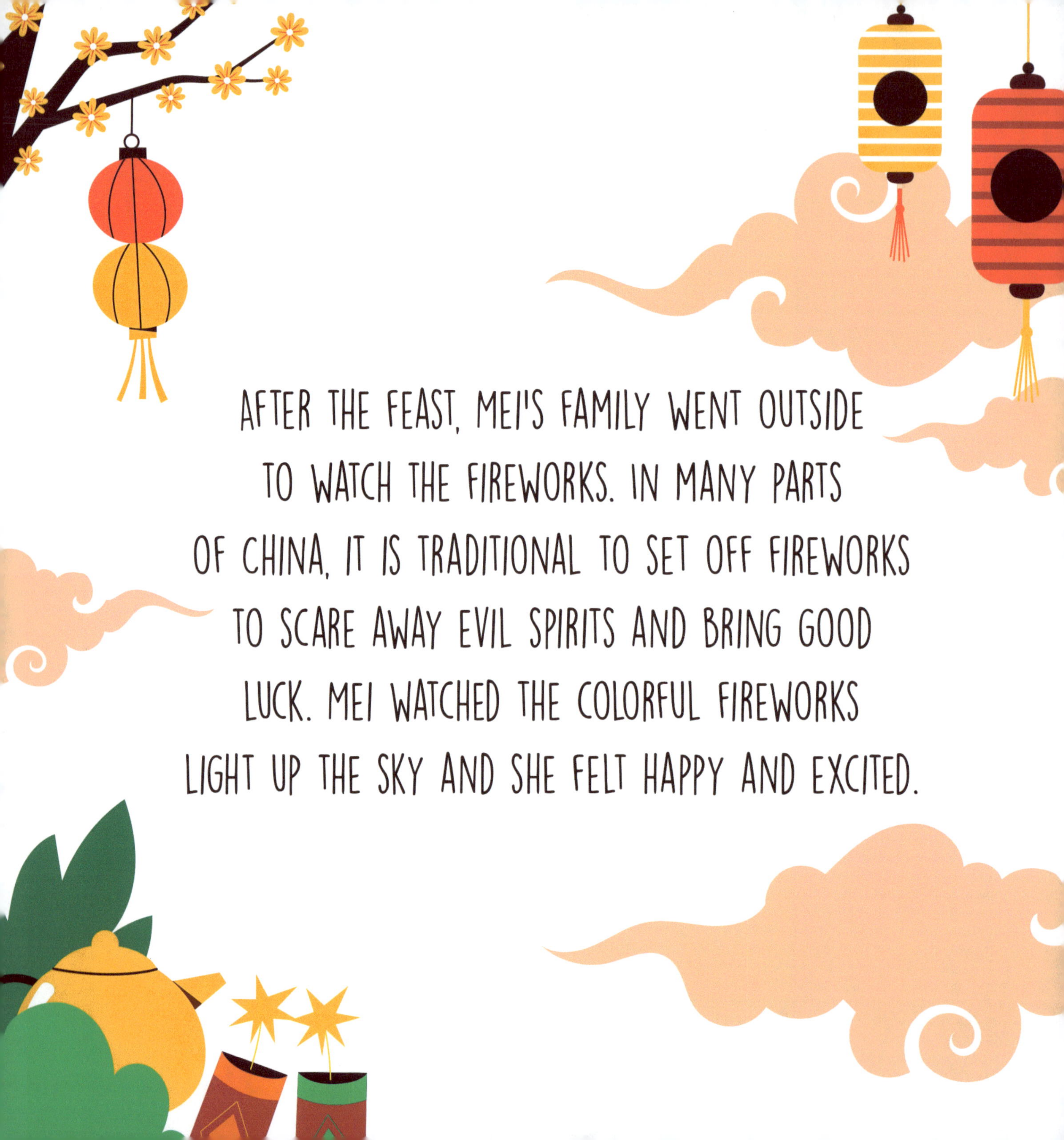

AFTER THE FEAST, MEI'S FAMILY WENT OUTSIDE TO WATCH THE FIREWORKS. IN MANY PARTS OF CHINA, IT IS TRADITIONAL TO SET OFF FIREWORKS TO SCARE AWAY EVIL SPIRITS AND BRING GOOD LUCK. MEI WATCHED THE COLORFUL FIREWORKS LIGHT UP THE SKY AND SHE FELT HAPPY AND EXCITED.

AS SHE ENJOYED THE CELEBRATIONS, MEI
TOOK A MOMENT TO REFLECT ON ALL
THE THINGS SHE WAS GRATEFUL FOR.
SHE THOUGHT ABOUT HER FAMILY, HER HOME,
AND ALL THE GOOD THINGS IN HER LIFE.
SHE WAS GRATEFUL FOR THE FOOD SHE HAD
EATEN AND FOR THE OPPORTUNITY TO
CELEBRATE WITH HER LOVED ONES.

CHINESE NEW YEAR IS A TIME FOR FAMILIES TO COME TOGETHER AND CELEBRATE THEIR CULTURAL HERITAGE.

IT IS ALSO A TIME TO REMEMBER THE
VALUES OF KINDNESS, RESPECT,
AND HARD WORK, WHICH ARE IMPORTANT
TO THE CHINESE PEOPLE.

MEI WAS GRATEFUL FOR ALL
THE GOOD THINGS IN HER LIFE
AND SHE HOPED FOR A HAPPY
AND PROSPEROUS NEW YEAR.

THE END.